Fit for the Chase

Fit for the Chase

Cars and the Movies

by Raymond Lee

CASTLE BOOKS ★ NEW YORK

To
Donald G. Dupree
and
B. C. Van Hecke

without whose help this book could
not have been compiled

Acknowledgments:

Academy of Motion Picture Arts and Sciences, Miss Lillian Schwartz and
    Staff
Classic Film Collector, Mr. Samuel K. Rubin, Publisher
Cecil B. De Mille Estate, Mrs. Cecilia Harper and Miss Florence Cole
Alpha Books, Mrs. Betty Vasin
Mr. Gabe Essoe, Disney Studios
Mrs. Minta Durfee Arbuckle
Mrs. Lillian Bernstein
Mrs. Dorothy Gibson
Clarence Sinclair Bull
Mrs. Eunice Friend
Mrs. Virginia Knight
Mrs. Stella Rae
Picture Car Co. Mr. James Brucker and Mr. Jerry Ross
Mr. Bob Pike
Mr. Manuel Weltman
Mr. and Mrs. Richard F. Main
John E. Allen, Inc.
Pat Jordan
James Zorich, Associate Curator Industrial Technology of Los Angeles
    Museum
For their generous help without which this book would have not been
    completed.

RAYMOND LEE

Contents

Fit for the Chase

1

How the Wheels Won

The automobile careened around the corner and headed straight for the audience. The first three rows emptied quicker than magician Houdini could finger-snap a disappearance. After much coaxing from the quick-thinking manager of the movie house that no one would be killed, the first three rows filled up again. He explained it was all make-believe and he proved his point by re-running the thrilling newsreel. Thunderous applause rocked the flicker palace.

Wheels were born and headed for cinema stardom as one of its greatest "props," rivaling even the horse for stunts, laughs and silent celluloid mayhem.

Daredevil serial queens Pearl White, Ruth Roland, and Helen Holmes crashed cars through walls and off cliffs; they sideswiped charging locomotives and escaped villains; they raised the blood pressure of film fans around the world.

The Keystone Cops, Charlie Chaplin, Harold Lloyd, Laurel and Hardy, W. C. Fields, and Harry Langdon with Vernon Dent turned the breakaway Ford into a tin pretzel that was the wildest caper in all comedydom.

Chaplin led the parade with *A Jitney Elopement* featuring the flivver while he tried to run off with beautiful Edna Purviance pursued by bad guy Leo White.

In 1919 *'Twas Henry's Fault* climaxed all the joking about the Tin Lizzie featuring Elinor Field and Harry Deep. As a star the Model T reached a unique peak which illustrated the madcap imagination of the pioneer producers.

Vamps Theda Bara, Louise Glaum and Virginia Pearson seduced innocent heroes on leopard-skinned couches; but the "It Girl," Clara Bow, and the "Dancing Darling," Joan Crawford—followed by the "Blonde Bombshell," Jean Harlow—topped the vamp's scores three times over by tumbling their boys in rumbles, and thus shook the 1920's through the 1940's from bumper to bumper.

The gangsters, led by Humphrey Bogart, James Cagney and Edward G. Robinson, didn't shoot from the hip as western stars William S. Hart, Tom Mix, and Hoot Gibson. They machine-gunned from screaming wheels that shocked the pants off both fan sexes.

But all on wheels wasn't violence.

Andy Hardy, or as some like to call him, Mickey Rooney, fell in love with cars and a few girls named Judy Garland, Ann Rutherford, and Lana Turner.

So the wheels spun and revved up every kind of emotion the silver screen could reflect.

What about the off-screen cars?

They drew headlines along with the off-screen romances of the human actors.

Many times when the Queen of Flaming Youth, Clara Bow, crooked her finger at three o'clock in the morning, an entire football team that was quite famous on its own, Southern California's "Thundering Herd," piled into Clara's open Kessel and charged up and down Hollywood Boulevard; and some remember stopping for a game of "touch" at Hollywood and Vine. Valentino thrilled fans on the famed street racing alternately his Isotta Fraschini and Avion Voisin—also during the wee hours. And Jean Harlow's black V-12 Cadillac raised temperatures from one end of filmland to the other.

The Pierce-Arrow became as popular as a climax in a shoot 'em up Horse Opera. A Rolls-Royce was in almost every driveway. Jackie Coogan kept two

at all times during his reign as the silent screen's most beloved kid star. A sidelight: it was his Daddy who brought the first Rolls agency to Southern California.

But Henry Ford saw to it that the Model-A wasn't outdone. It was American and Americans would come to love it as its heart-car no matter how many thousands of dollars were spent on overseas custom-mades. Producer-Director Cecil B. DeMille, who had at his disposal a bevy of the most expensive wheels of the day, loved his 1928 sedan. Douglas Fairbanks and Mary Pickford drove the first coupe down Hollywood Boulevard from their Beverly Hills Mansion known as "Pickfair." Mexican star Dolores Del Rio didn't lose any of her glamor driving a Model-A.

As a gossip columnist quipped in '29: "A Ford isn't a stream anymore—at least in movieland . . ." The automobile was involved in many "Firsts."

A camera mounted on the back seat of a Thomas Studio car inspired some of Cecil B. De Mille's most exciting silents.

Hoot Gibson, considered the top horseman of all the Western stars, won the World Championship at Pendleton, Oregon in 1912 before trekking to Hollywood, and was the first to bull-dog a steer from a car.

A tragic first: Tom Mix, hailed as the most terrific cowboy in the world—he had fought in the Chinese Boxer Rebellion, had been a Texas Ranger, and had started as a guard with gun in hand in wild animal films—lost his life to his second greatest love on a lonely Arizona road in 1940.

The wheel is embedded deep in America's tradition. It all started with the Covered Wagon—sweeping away frontiers, banging up and down mountains, forging across raging torrents and whirling deserts to reach the Pacific ocean.

But man wanted more speed in his race against time. The train took up the challenge and rolled and tunnelled its way and carried people and baggage to places that didn't even have names. In 1903 pioneer producer Edwin S. Porter with *The Great Train Robbery* immortalized the locomotive and brought maturity to the infant flicker.

Someone took a look at the bicycle, put powered speed on it, and produced a death-defying web of spinning wind and swirling dust.

But the rider didn't always want to be alone and in the automobile he found togetherness along with speed.

In the film of John Steinbeck's classic novel, *Grapes of Wrath*, this togetherness reached a peak that almost approached Greek tragedy. The quest of the Joad family to find roots—their flight in the battered, beaten, and besieged old jalopy in search of a new horizon—symbolized a struggle for survival rare in America's history plus it illustrated the plight of the Great Depression's "poverty stricken" and showed how wheels gave hope to the few who lived through the ordeal.

Who starred the first car?

One hot summer afternoon in 1913 Mack Sennett strode grim-faced from a session with his gag-men, who had come up with not one gag in two sweating hours. He treated those bums like kings: He had built them their own bungalow, and had given them every luxury except booze, which he forbade anyone on the Keystone Lot to indulge in though he suspected his writers guzzled behind his back.

Standing in the blinding sunlight he was suddenly involved in one of the many fancies he was famous for, and which had helped him to be crowned King of Comedy. No one ever knew when or how these vagaries would smack Mack but something always shook the fun factory like a bomb.

He surveyed the studio. He always thought of the comforts of his actors and directors—and writers. He had built them a swimming pool. Sometimes they were in it more than they were before his cameras. But what about himself? Sennett sat in a stuffy office that should have belonged to the janitor. He slapped his thigh and shouted to two assistants:

"No more! No more will the King reign like a pauper!"

Barging into the prop shop like his favorite Lion actor, Numa, he roared out orders for building a two-storied administration building which would be topped by a tower—his own personal tower. As the shopboss just stared he roared his loudest:

"Its got to be a tower from which I can see every square foot of the lot, even what the mice are stealing. A tower from which I'll conduct my conferences in the biggest bathtub in Hollywood!"

Measuring eight feet from stem to stern—six feet of beam and drawing five feet—it shone like a jewel in the center of the tower. A small desk stood in a corner to make the room official.

As King Mack, lathered from head to toe, one morning addressed his gagsters from the Gargantuan marble trough:

"In the morning it's a diamond. A sunset. A ruby. If I ever bathe at full moon I am sure it will turn into a pearl. Now, what the hell else kind of inspiring do you blokes need?"

About to sink under a wave of scented suds, he popped a bubble from his palms.

"Boys, this is Abdul. Abdul these are the boys. He's in charge of the gym over there and every last one of you has to work out with him or I'll cancel out every contract!"

Abdul the Turk. A tower of a man. A name long remembered by every comedy writer in the Sennett menagerie. He exercised them until they could hardly walk. He steamed them in the chamber until they looked like over-ripe tomatoes. He rubbed them down with salt until they bled. But he sobered up their beered-bodies while King Mack sharpened their minds with fancies.

It was mad but it was movies—and Mack Sennett for real and on reel—and it worked like magic. The gags rocked out of the tower and the world had its biggest belly laughs.

During one of the madcap bathcapades the King was strangely silent, his head bowed; Pepper, the alley-cat he'd made a star, was perched on his shoulder eating whipped cream from a dish held by Abdul.

Was the King sick? In love? Going to abdicate?

Slowly Mack lifted his head and stared at his laugh-making cortege.

"Fellows, you've been wonderful. I know I beat and kick you around but always we seem to come up with a laugh."

Many "yeses" from the crew.

"But suddenly I feel we're walking in a swamp. The custard pie was a beautiful gag. But how many pies can you throw, and for how long?"

The silence was deep enough to hear Pepper lapping her whipped cream.

"Is this the end of the greatest laugh factory in the world? Is it fellows?"

Gloom enveloped the Tower, broken only by the plop of scented salts dropped in the massive tub by Abdul.

There was not even a puff on a cigarette or an itch to scratch. No one seemed even to breathe.

Suddenly, like King Neptune, the King rose in the tub; his eyes were fixed on the ceiling.

"'As if a wheel had been in the midst of a wheel . . .'"

He looked around for reaction.

"Ezekiel Chapter 10 . . . Verse 10 . . ."

The fellows exchanged looks as if they were marked cards. "The King is quoting from the Bible for laughs," someone whispered. Another crossed himself. A third suggested they call a doctor. But no one moved; they just watched.

The King was now soap-robed and never looked more regal in his life. He held Pepper like a sceptre in his right arm. Suddenly the warm air dried him stark naked.

"It's funny, you dopes. Lots of comedy

in the Bible. Just have to look for it. The wheel was a hero who rescued man from slavery. Now the wheel will be the villain that traps and torments him but doesn't really hurt him."

A gagster jumped to his feet.

"The Tin Lizzie loaded with cops chasing robbers between two trolley cars."

"And sandwiched like cheese!"

"Bullying a locomotive at a crossing and losing its tail!"

"Fording a lake like only a Ford can!"

The King slid back into his massive indoor yacht, Abdul poured more whipped cream for Pepper, then began to rub the back of his majesty's neck as the cortege whirled and danced and laughed.

As the bedlam subsided:

"Mack, however did you think about the Bible?"

A faraway look was in the King's eyes.

"My Mama used to read the Bible at night. And that passage about the wheel stuck in my head. I laughed the first time she read it. And Mama slapped me. How could I forget it?"

Below the Tower there was a bang and a backfire. Everyone including Mack rushed to the windows. Below, a Tin Lizzie driven by a girl with long black curls burst through the studio gates.

Mack smiled.

"Its Mabel doing what will now come naturally for all our stars."

Dust swirled high and two of the King's greatest stars, Mabel Normand and the Tin Lizzie took off for parts unknown . . .

Mack Sennett (seated), Vernon Dent (Rear), and Syd Smith (at right) watch the Tower being constructed on the world's greatest laugh lot in 1913.

Cowboy star Hoot Gibson and Co. in 1919 Packard.

Rudolph Valentino's European-built Avion Voisin (French) 1925.

18

Edward G. Robinson gives Buster Collier some gangster advice in *Little Caesar*. The car is a 1926 Cadillac Touring model.

Whenever there was a Hollywood premiere a long line of classic cars would roll up. This one was the first double feature: Mary Pickford in *Sparrows* and Douglas Fairbanks in *The Black Pirate*.

C. B. DeMille and the first Model-A Ford (a 1928 sedan) at his Culver City studio.

Joan Crawford and admirers enjoy a 1929 Pierce Arrow.

Adolphe Menjou tempts Constance Bennett with a 1930 Cadillac, which introduced the V-16 engine. The car, which cost over $8,000, is today considered a true classic.

James Cagney takes his lumps in *Each Dawn I Die* while Stuart Holmes watches. The blood is being spilled on a 1930 Nash Ambassador.

Jean Harlow is stepping into her 1934
V-12 Cadillac town car.

Driving a 1930 Model-A Ford, Humphrey Bogart faces up to gangster Cliff
Young in *Dark Passage*.

The Joad family head for California
in John Ford's classic, *The Grapes of
Wrath*.

Laraine Day (in dark dress) and Mary Howard (with polka dot dress) set out to see chief points of interest in Hollywood, driving a 1939 Packard, in the days when they both starred for MGM.

Life Begins for Andy Hardy in a 1941 Plymouth. Mickey Rooney and Judy Garland are the occupants.

2

Everybody Loves a Tin Lizzie

Millions of words have been written about the antics of the flivvers and Chaplin, Laurel and Hardy, W. C. Fields, Harry Langdon, and the Keystone Cops.

But words can never describe "looking" at their madcapping . . .

The Keystone Kops stand in review in front of a 1910 Model T Ford.

This 1912 Model T Ford is headed for trouble, with the Keystone Kops inside.

The Kops in a special Breakaway Ford.

The Kops kaper in this mock-up Tin Lizzie, in *Hollywood Cavalcade*.

In *The Passionate Plumber,* Buster
Keaton and Jimmy Durante take a stand-
up ride in this 1914 Model T touring
Ford.

Charlie Chaplin and his family are
Out for a Day's Pleasure in this 1914
Model T touring Ford. Behind them is a
1917 Smith Farm Truck.

Tommy Steele and Lesley Ann Warren laugh it up before a 1915 Model T. The film is Disney's *Happiest Millionaire*. (© MCMLXVI by Walt Disney Productions)

In *The Barnstormers*, a William Fox "Sunshine" Comedy, a 1913 Model T is pitted against a 1917 Winton 6.

Eddie Gribbon and Eddie Lyons in a
Keystone Comedy. The Car is a 1914
Model T.

Eileen Percy is *The Husband Hunter*
in front of the 1914 Model T.

Fred MacMurray takes off in a 1915
Model T in *Son of Flubber* . . . (© *Walt
Disney Productions*)

. . . And Fred takes to the sky
again in *The Absent-Minded Professor*.
(© MCMLXII Walt Disney Productions)

Hank Mann (left) and Vernon Dent run into problems with this 1917 Model T. (The front fenders, windshield, and headlights have been removed.)

Vernon and Hank again, in front of a 1917 Model T pickup. (Hank is on the left.)

Jimmy Finlayson tears up a 1919 Model T Ford roadster converted into a pickup truck as Laurel and Hardy look on.

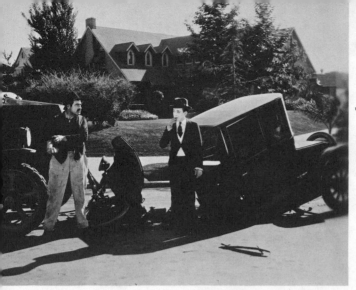

Harry Langdon beside a 1919 Model
T coupe and Bull Dog Mack Truck.

Laurel and Hardy tear up a 1919
Model T in *Two Tars*.

Richard Dix has problems with his
1920 Model T touring car.

Keystone Kops recall zany days of
old in 1921 Model T Ford.

1923 Model T serves up laughs for
Laurel and Hardy.

W. C. Fields tells off kid in 1923
Model T. The film is *It's the Old Army
Game*.

Gabby Hayes and Monte Hale in 1924
Model T touring car.

Nino Martini and Leo Carillo enjoy a laugh with a 1924 Model T touring car (left) and 1920 center-door Ford (right).

A lamp post ends Laurel and Hardy's trip in their 1923 Model T roadster.

Laurel and Hardy are still breaking things up in their 1924 Model T. That's a 1927 Page in the background (rear, right).

Laurel and Hardy ponder the consequences of their mishap. They are riding in a special breakaway Model T.

Polly Moran, Cliff Edwards, and Marie Dressler (at wheel) in MGM's *Hollywood Revue*. The Car is a 1924 Ford touring car.

Laurel and Hardy salute in a 1924 Model T.

No, not every Tin Lizzie could do this trick. But Laurel and Hardy are driving a special breakaway model (1924).

The Three Stooges cavort with the aid of a 1926 Model T.

In this scene from *Giant,* Liz Taylor and James Dean ride in a 1926 Ford pickup.

Beautiful Vilma Banky brightens up a 1928 Model T.

W. C. Fields checks the mail; baby Leroy looks on. The car is a 1929 Model A Ford.

Harold Lloyd fights to stay out of 1930
Model A Phaeton.

George Sidney and Charles Murray
in *The Cohens and the Kelleys*. Left:
1936 Star. Right: 1931 Ford pickup.

3

Suit the Wheels to the Action, the Action to the Wheels

Paraphrasing Shakespeare most writers will say is the kiss of death. But wasn't Death the immortal Bard's real star?

And so it was in movies.

Serial queens pursued by villains . . . gangsters machine-gunning friend and foe alike . . . the jazz-agers mixing gin and gas as though they were twins . . .

If the Man from Avon had known wheels he surely would have made throne-lusting MacBeth dispose of the King by hiding a bomb under the starter of his royal wagon rather than with a bloody stabbing . . .

Rock Hudson in spectacular crash for *The Earth is Mine.*

A 1904 Rambler is the center of attention here.

A horse versus a 1907 Thomas Flyer. Tom Mix directs traffic.

Polly Moran, Renee Adoree, and Conrad Nagel make their escape in a 1914 International Harvester Truck in the World War I Epic, *Heaven on Earth*.

Ben Johnson gets to the rescue of Candy Moore ahead of a 1924 Model T in this scene from *Tomboy and the Champ*.

Leatrice Joy has a close call with a train in her 1921 Hudson. The dog is Teddy. The film is Cecil B. De Mille's *Manslaughter*.

Richard Dix, in his 1921 Rolls Royce, comes to the aid of a 1924 Packard in a scene shot on the Mojave Desert.

William Russell pulls a stickup in a 1919 Stutz; his victims have been forced to get out of their 1917 Pierce Arrow.

Robert Blake makes a reluctant exit from his 1926 Pierce Arrow in *The Purple Gang*.

A 1927 Cadillac is the scene for this
episode of *The Dummy*.

A 1927 Lincoln finds itself in the middle of a gun battle in *Portrait of a Mob-
ster*.

Gangsters prepare for action in De Mille's *This Day and Age*. They are driving a 1927 Lincoln.

Rudolph Valentino (Anthony Dexter) accepts a ride from the studio offered by Lila Reyes (Patricia Medina) in her brand new 1927 Pierce Arrow roadster. This scene is from Columbia Pictures' *Valentino*.

A below-the-border lynching party gathers around a 1929 Rolls Royce Phaeton as they listen to Leo Carrillo urge them on.

Gene Autry and Smiley Burnette seem to be in trouble with the law in *Gaucho Serenade*. Our cowboy heroes are in a 1929 Studebaker. The cop's 1936 Faro Police Car is parked alongside.

This scene from *Stranger's Return* features Lionel Barrymore, Stu Erwin, and a 1929 Studebaker.

The Purple Gang removes a body from a 1930 Pierce Arrow.

A 1930 Cadillac is the scene for a meeting between Jean Harlow and James Cagney in *Public Enemy*. Edward Woods ogles Jean.

Alan Ladd is at the wheel of this 1931 Packard Dual-Coil Phaeton in this scene from *The Great Gatsby*. Shelly Winters is doing a little gassing herself, with Howard Da Silva.

This fight scene from *Wild River* is staged between (left to right) a 1931 Model A Ford, a 1929 Plymouth, and a 1934 De Soto Air Flow. That's a 1935 Chevrolet truck in the foreground.

That's a Model B Ford truck going
over the side of *The Mountain Road*.

This is a scene from Columbia's All
Star Comedy #457. The stars are Noah
Beery, Jr., Shemp Howard, and Paul
Hurst. Their car is a very rare 1933
Model C Ford.

The Model C was also featured in this scene from *Hoedown*, with Jock O'Mahoney, Jeff Donnell, and Eddy Arnold.

Gene Autry runs down a 1936 Ford in *Blue Montana Skies*.

Clark Gable and Myrna Loy use the top of a 1940 Dodge in this scene from *Too Hot to Handle*.

A 1937 Packard serves as a shield for
Ma Barker's Killer Brood.

An International Fire Truck makes the
scene in *The Housekeeper's Daughter*.
That's a 1937 Ford in the foreground.

Tom Ellis is bid farewell by this 1937 Plymouth.

John Mills gets out of his 1937 Rolls to hunt for a body in *Mr. Denning Drives North*.

A 1938 Chrysler is stopping for Mickey Rooney, who is running away from *Boys Town*.

The Joads enter Keene Ranch in this scene from *The Grapes of Wrath*—unaware that they have been hired as strikebreakers.

Tony Britton (left) and Peter Finch take cover behind a 1938 Mercedes in *Operation Amsterdam*.

Douglas Fairbanks is being chauffered to the scene in *The Great Manhunt*.

Behind a 1941 Cadillac, Constance Bennett trades flashlights with Kur Kreuger in *Guerrillas of the Underground.*

Barry Fitzgerald lies critically injured after having been run over by a 1941 Dodge. Sonny Tufts and Diana Lynn look on, in this scene from *Easy Come, Easy Go*.

This *was* a 1941 Oldsmobile. Burt Lancaster watches as medics try to save John Hodiak in *Desert Fury*.

George Sanders is *The Saint in London*.

Guns Don't Argue, especially when held by cigar-puffing ladies in Cadillacs (1941).

Spencer Tracy uses 1942 Ford Jeep as a shield in this shoot-out from *Bad Day at Black Rock*.

David Wayne hustles the protesting Paul Muni into a waiting 1947 Buick in *The Last Angry Man*.

A 1953 Jaguar Mark 7 hides murdered and murderer in *Twist of Fate.*

All is not quiet for Audie Murphy and Michael Redgrave in *The Quiet American.*

Cars on fire are always an eerie sight, especially when combined with the horrors of war, as in this sequence from *The Quiet American.*

1948 Chevrolet truck battles Rhino
with help from John Wayne in *Hatari*.

Is he really dead? The police, in *The Rebel Set* aren't taking any chances. The last ride was taken in a 1949 Cadillac.

This is a scene from *Speed Crazy*. The cars are a 1954 Austin Healey (left) and a 1954 Porcshe (right). The girl is Yvonne Lime.

A 1957 Ford police car takes Frank Sinatra for a ride in *The Man with the Golden Arm*.

Paul Newman calls for the driver of 1958 Dodge pickup to help in *Hud*.

Leslie Caron and David Niven try to
make it from the swamp in which their
1957 Ford Station Wagon is sinking in
Guns of Darkness.

A 1957 Ford serves as a shield in
Tokyo After Dark.

Frank Sinatra and Peter Lawford come to the aid of John Conte—sandwiched between a 1958 Thunderbird and a 1958 Mercedes—after daring casino robbery in *Ocean's Eleven*.

A 1961 Chevrolet has brought injury in *Cape Fear*.

A 1959 Jeep, a 1950 Chevrolet Truck—
and John Wayne—in this scene from
Hatari.

Steve McQueen demands a little ex-
planation in *Soldier in the Rain*. Vehicles
are a 1961 Thunderbird and a Chevrolet
army truck.

1962 Oldsmobile stirs up plenty of dust in *Desire in the Dust*.

Classic cars and Texans gather for barbecue in *Giant*. Left to right: Two Rolls Royces, a Duesenberg, and a Lincoln.

4

Anything for a Laugh

Because the word "anything" heads three chapters non-students of semantics might appreciate a dictionary's view:

"1. Anything whatever; something, no matter what. 2. a thing of any kind. 3. in any degree; to any extent. 4. anything but, in no degree or respect; not in the least. The plans were anything but definite."

Sounds like a fun word. And a fair description of laughter. You laugh inside or out. You rarely laugh alone; you laugh with hundreds of people in crowds or a theatre. You laugh at calamity that doesn't harm.

The great comics never defined their art. They left that Herculean task to the critics. But they tried anything for a laugh, bruising muscles and bones and other things.

Anything . . . something . . . to any extent . . .

Charley Butterworth demonstrates correct method of driving horseless carriages in this sequence from *Every Day's a Holiday*.

P2056-31

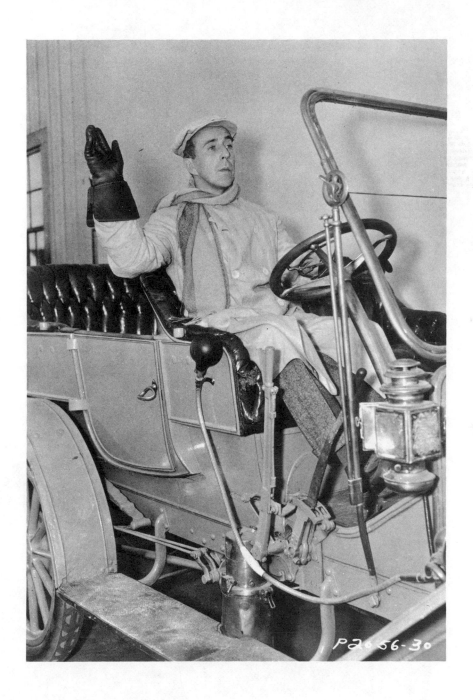

Scenes from *The Great Race*, featuring Tony Curtis, Jack Lemmon, and Natalie Wood, plus the Eiffel Tower and some very unusual cars.

It's a draw as to who suffered the worst injury in this Vernon Dent silent.

A squealing success is what Johnny Hines expects to make in *Rainbow Riley*. Here he is seen with four of the reasons, and his charming leading lady, Brenda Bond. The car is a 1902 Curved-Dash Oldsmobile.

Marion Davies and Lawrence Gray go for a ride in a 1904 Oldsmobile, with straight dash.

A 1905 one-cylinder Reo was used for this early short.

Ed Wynn drives a 1907 Sears in *The Fire Chief*.

The cast of *I Remember Mama* are
assembled in a 1909 Mitchell.

Tyrone Power and Maureen O'Hara
look over this 1909 Four-cylinder Touring Cadillac.

Richard Delmer is at the wheel of a
1912 Marmon sports roadster.

This 1914 Model T has ended up in a
dress shop in a 1917 Keystone comedy.
Charles Murray is at the wheel; Louise
Fazenda is on the motorcycle.

Leo Gorcey in a scene from *The Bow-
ery Boys*. That's a 1914 Tin Lizzie that
appears to need adjustments.

John Davidson serenades Lesley Ann Warren in Disney's *The Happiest Millionaire*. The car is a 1916 Mercedes raceabout. (© MCMLXVI by Walt Disney Productions)

"Hands off my Columbia," says Hank Mann to Vernon Dent. (It's a 1920 model.)

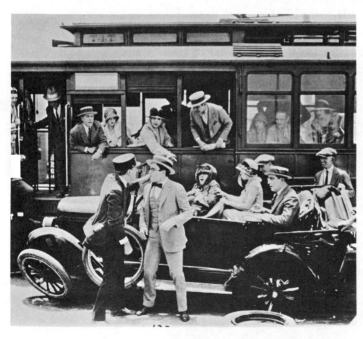

It is doubtful if either Harold Lloyd or his 1921 Chevrolet will last much longer. These scenes are from *Harold Lloyd's World of Comedy.*

Thelma Hill, Vernon Dent, Bill Bevan,
a lot of mud, and a 1921 Essex.

Wrong gear, slapstick style. (The car
is an English Austin.)

A 1922 Cadillac is coming apart at
the seams in Hal Roach's *You're Telling
Me*.

Vernon Dent and Hank Mann in front
of a 1922 Nash.

Wallace Beery and Raymond Hatton
help the lady out of a 1923 Cole.

Raymond Griffith and William Powell have back seat problems with their 1924 MacFarland.

Our Gang is in *Tire Trouble* (1924).

Clarence the Cross-Eyed Lion hitches a ride with Richard Hayden in his 1925 Model T.

With slightly tipsey Harry Meyers at the wheel, Charlie Chaplin goes for a wild ride in a 1925 Rolls Royce in his classic *City Lights*.

A picnic lunch in a Hal Roach comedy. The party arrived in a 1925 Rolls Royce.

Safety First? This 1925 Willys St. Clair has apparently disregarded the sign.

Richard Dix with 1926 Chevrolet in
early silent on Mojave Desert.

Richard Dix tries to take an elderly
gentleman for his first ride, in a 1926
Packard, in this scene from *Easy Come,
Easy Go.*

Wallace Beery and Raymond Hatton
hitching a ride from a 1927 Packard.

In this scene from *The Meanest Gal in
Town*, Zazu Pitts and Ed Brendel use a
1928 Model A for their negotiating table.

Some people will get married anywhere, as Vernon Dent and Duane
Thompson prove.

Joe E. Brown tries to free his 1928
Rolls from difficulties.

Laurel and Hardy are stuck in a traffic
jam, which they seem to be responsible
for.

Leon Errol and Vince Barnett in a
scene from *One Heavenly Night*. A 1928
Rolls Royce plays a supporting role.

Jackie Cooper tries to explain trolley
trouble to passengers of a 1929 Cadillac.

Trouble of the sort that only Polly
Moran and Marie Dressler could get
into. The action is centered about a
1929 Cadillac.

This old Model A Ford (1929) is so
unused to being fed gasoline that it back-
fires and frightens Huntz Hall, Gabriel
Dell, and Bernard Punsly (obscured by
the smoke) in this episode of *Mug Town*.

Marion Davies is having her problems
in a 1930 American Austin.

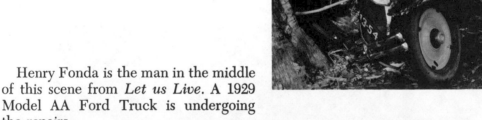

Henry Fonda is the man in the middle
of this scene from *Let us Live*. A 1929
Model AA Ford Truck is undergoing
the repairs.

W. C. Fields never walks where he can ride, as he demonstrates in *The 300 Yard Drive*. A 1930 American Bantam is saving him steps.

Majorie Main and Percy Kilbride are the immortal Ma and Pa Kettle. Their 1931 Model A seems to be holding its own against the train.

Youth takes over where horsepower fails, as Vera Miles gets rolling under the steam of Fred MacMurray and his group of campers in Disney's *Follow Me, Boys*. The car is a 1931 Lincoln. (© MCMLXV by Walt Disney Productions)

Vernon Dent seems to be trying to beat his 1932 Buick to death.

W. C. Fields warns blind man in this scene from *If I Had a Million*. His 1932 Model B Ford is a very rare vehicle.

Rosalind Russell and Robert Donat in *The Citadel*. The truck is a 1932 Ford, Model BB.

Walt Disney's *Gnome Mobile* is in reality a 1932 Rolls. Walter Brennan is at the wheel. (© MCMLXVI by Walt Disney Productions)

Seeing is Believing. Stuart Erwin is both the boss and the chauffeur. The car is a 1934 Cadillac.

Merrily we Live, says Jimmy Stewart to Constance Bennett, behind the wheel of a 1935 Duesenberg.

Where is the door of this 1936 Buick? The cast of *About Face* would certainly like to know.

Vernon Dent's 1936 Ford is being polished. Perhaps the fact that the Three Stooges are doing the job is cause for the concerned look on his face.

Well, Buster, what do you expect from
a woman driver? (1939 Dodge.)

Gene Autry and June Storey discuss
reason for the unscheduled washing for
the 1940 Hudson, in *Gaucho Serenade*.

Cast of *Joe Butterfly*, starring Audie Murphy and George Nader, pose in this jeep.

Cecil Kellaway decides to see if *The Luck of the Irish* will work with the constabulary. Tyrone Power wonders, too. The car is a 1946 Lincoln.

The Two Little Bears are being corralled in this 1948 MG TC.

Rosalind Russell and Robert Cummings are the newlyweds in *Tell it To the Judge*. Their 1949 Ford is ready for the winter weather.

Jack Carson looks on in disbelief at the wreckage on *Rally Round the Flag, Boys*. Dodge makes the Army's trucks.

A T. Bucket Hot Rod is having some difficulties in *Dragstrip Girl*.

A zebra is upstaging the Land Rover in *Serengeti*.

Jerry Lewis is bugged by a Bug in *The Bellboy*.

This strange vehicle, from *Eegah,* is called a Dunebuggy.

5

Anything for a Thrill

The movie stuntman first won his spurs on horseback. On wheels he sometimes lost his life. A unique breed of daredevil, his head-on crashes, dives off cliffs, and flaming somersaults earned him a special "Oscar" in the hearts of all thrill-lovers . . .

"The Skywayman," Lt. Amer Locklear
was killed in this scene.

Here are two more shots of "The Sky-wayman" in action as he circles a church.

This revamped prop Hupmobile gets the Keystone Kops into difficulty.

Art Lee is ready to leap on the heavyweight champion of the world, Jim Corbett, in early serial.

A British Army vehicle is an important factor in this sequence from *Drums of Fu Manchu*.

Harold Lloyd is in difficulties again, this time with a fire truck.

Wallace Berry and Raymond Hatton
battle in front of this Stutz fire truck.

Feminine charms prove futile in *The
Blind Goddess.*

Helene Chadwick and Harry Meyers seem to be having some success with this officer.

Famed stuntman Joe Bonomo shows why he was tops in his field.

Queen of the Serials Pearl White always did her own stunting. The overturned auto is a 1912 Simplex.

Villain Henry Pemberton throws chauffeur out in *Trade Secret*, a 1914 serial.

Hal Cooley and Gertrude Olmstead run their 4-cylinder 1916 Dodge into a tree and get bruised for their art.

Francis X. Bushman also did his own
stunting. That's a 1917 Reo about to be
crushed.

Yakima Canutt, one of the greatest
stunters, uses horses and wheels for a
leap in *Zorro Rides Again*. Canutt may
not know it, but he is about to go for
a ride in a Sterling Truck.

A 1927 Chevrolet encounters a 1932 truck in this scene from *Burn 'Em Up Barnes*.

Again difficulties with the law: Ralph Graves is in the 1926 Chrysler; Vernon Dent is on the four-cylinder Henderson motorcycle.

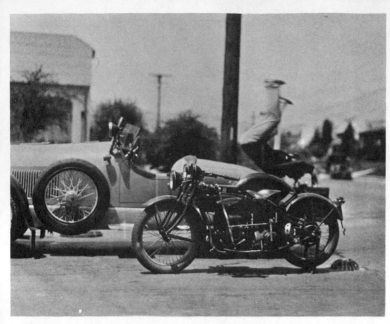

Richard Talmadge leaps from Indian
Motorcycle into a 1927 Jordan Playboy.

Richard Talmadge leaps off a building
in this sequence.

Carole Lombard and Zazu Pitts try to
smile away the police.

Charles Hutchinson leaps into 1927
Hutchinson in *Hidden Aces*. Leaps like
this were his specialty.

Who'll make it to the crossing first? Charles Hutchinson is at the wheel of the 1928 Lincoln, with Alice Calhoun beside him.

Everyone seems to be ignoring the 1931 Packard in *Daredevils of the Red Circle*.

Action near explosive material is always a suspense-builder, as in this scene from *Daredevils of the Red Circle*.

A getaway scene from *Daredevils of the Red Circle*. A 1934 Cadillac kicks up the dust.

A leap onto a 1939 Ford Standard Station Wagon, in this scene from *Daredevils of the Red Circle*.

A 1937 Ford Station Wagon has turned over.

The lady is in trouble in *Destiny*. She
is driving a 1937 Plymouth.

Rex Allen takes a shortcut over a 1946
Buick on Koko, "Miracle Horse of the
Movies," in *Rodeo King and the Seno-
rita*.

The 1953 Chevrolet has *A Date with Death*.

The 1954 Kaiser and the Harley-Davidson don't get on well in *Hot Car Girl*. June Kenney seems upset, as well she might be.

6

Anything Can Happen in a Taxicab

A beautiful blonde tripped from a taxicab; her dress caught in the door; and she was escorted into the lobby of a fashionable hotel with all her underthings showing. Her escorts were doormen played by Laurel and Hardy in a two-reeler titled *Double Whoopee*. The blonde? Her name was Jean Harlow. The year was 1928 and the most fabulous sex queen of the Thirties had taken her first step to stardom with a slapsick routine from the greatest comedy team of all time.

Joan Crawford in 1927's *The Taxi Driver* gained stature as a leading lady.

Red Skelton scored a hit starring as the man in front of the meter in 1950's *The Yellow Cab Man*.

And who can forget the thrilling scenes of the taxicabs of Paris carrying their soldiers to the front to stop the German onslaught in World War One's masterpiece, *Seventh Heaven?*

So the pay-for-the-ride-wheels had a good run of the gamut of cinema emotions even if they didn't get top billing . . .

Mickey Rooney in *A Yank at Eton*.

Allen Jenkins makes excuses to pretty passenger.

Billy Bevan (left) and Vernon De plot mischief with cab as third party.

Ben Blue gets a hug from a pretty passenger.

Charlie Chase frowns on attempts at free rides.

Jean Harlow, with Laurel and Hardy, made history stepping from a Yellow Cab in the 1928 two-reeler, *Double Whoopee.*

Harlow exits from Yellow Cab after door closes on skirt.

Bert Wheeler, Robert Woolsey, Kittey
Kelley, and supporting player in *Girl
Crazy*.

Love and Learn showed that there
were many uses for a taxi.

Harold Lloyd makes his getaway.

In *Partners in Crime*, Raymond Hatton uses a taxi to find old friends.

Harry Langdon (right) and Vernon
Dent have unloading problems.

Mary Astor receives, in the name of
Columbia studios, a letter from the
Mayor of Los Angeles to Grace Moore
in honor of her remarkable performance
in *The King Steps Out*. The letter was
delivered by Mr. Pedigo, Vice-President
of the Yellow Cab Company, and the
Fanchon and Marco girls from the Paramount Theater.

Eddie Cantor solicits riders for a trip to the homes of the stars.

In *Maid's Night Out*, the passenger getting out of the 1936 De Soto tips his hat to the lovely driver of a 1931 International Truck.

Taxi, European style.

Brian Donlevy tracks suspects in cab.

The Three Stooges cavort beside a 1939 Buick cab in *Stop! Look! and Laugh!*

Red Skelton stars as *The Yellow Cab Man*.

Bob Hope sees Paris in a Renault cab in *Paris Holiday*.

Clark Gable tips the doorman in this scene from *The Hucksters*. (The cab is a 1946 De Soto.)

The gunman doesn't make it to the Subway in *Side Street*. The cab is a 1946 De Soto; the cops are driving 1949 Fords.

Alan Ladd had many adventures in and out of cabs, like this 1946 Plymouth.

Jack Palance and Anita Ekberg alight from European cab in *The Man Inside*.

Debbie Reynolds puts charm in a meter-car (a 1955 Plymouth) in *The Rat Race*.

A fast way to enter a speeding cab. (A 1959 Plymouth.)

No law against a dog paying his way. (A 1961 Ford.)

A 1964 Ford has gone astray.

7

Life Is a Race

"But what minutes! Count them by sensation, and not by calendars, and each moment is a day, and the race a life . . ."

A pretty good description of the speed demons. Disraeli, while serving as Prime Minster of England, scribbled these lines one day while watching the "Sport of Kings" . . .

Burn 'em Up Barnes was a rare film that has never been equalled for sheer madness. First produced as a 12-episode serial in 1934, it was an instant hit. Later, in 1935, it was released as a 75-minute feature—and flopped. No one knows quite why the audience was so fickle. This capitol-steps sequence and the following photographs are all from this thriller.

Stars Jack Mulhall and Lola Lane on the track in a Model T Hooker special.

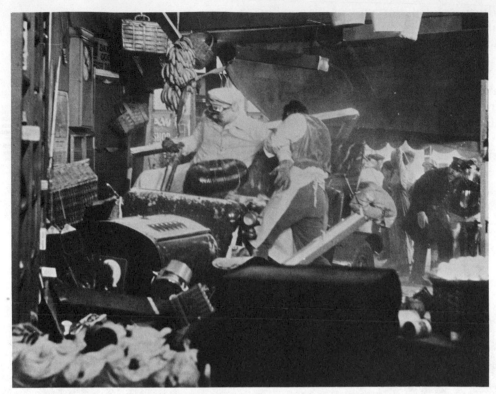

A 1905 Franklin finds itself in trouble.

A Model T in hot pursuit of a 1906 Packard.

A 2931 K-B Lincoln makes a turn.

A racer needs assistance from a truck.

Cars prepare for race in front of the
deserted stands.

Three of the adventurers ride into town.

The start of a New York to Paris race.

These photographs depict a series of
racers from MGM's famed 1930 short.

135

Leslie Banks is the early auto-club member.

A scene from *Race Caper*, an early Christie Comedy.

Racer, from an early silent.

Jimmy Cagney agrees to back Eric Linden in *The Crowd Roars*.

Clark Gable in a before-the-race interview with Barbara Stanwyck in *To Please a Lady*.

Gable at the wheel in *To Please a Lady*.

Rex Harrison in a scene from *The
Notorious Gentleman.*

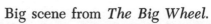

Big scene from *The Big Wheel.*

Mickey Rooney ready to take off in
The Big Wheel.

Hoot Gibson and Roger Ward race
Hoot's car at Indianapolis.

A draw, in *Ghost of Dragstrip Hollow.*

Tony Curtis, in two scenes from
Johnny Dark.

A spectacular crash in *On the Beach*.

A highlight of *Roadracers*.

A human triangle in *Roadracers*.

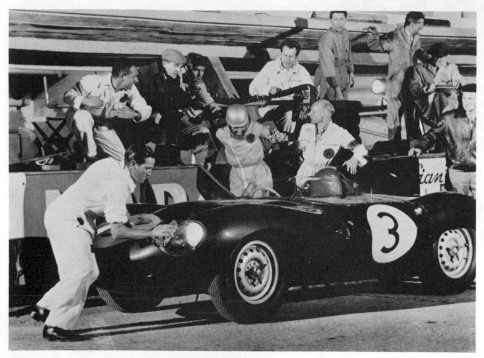

An emergency in *The Green Helmet*.

Ed Begley (center) talks with his drivers in *The Green Helmet*.

Basil Travers checks an engine in *The Green Helmet*.

Kirk Douglas and Lee J. Cobb talk over the race in *The Racers*.

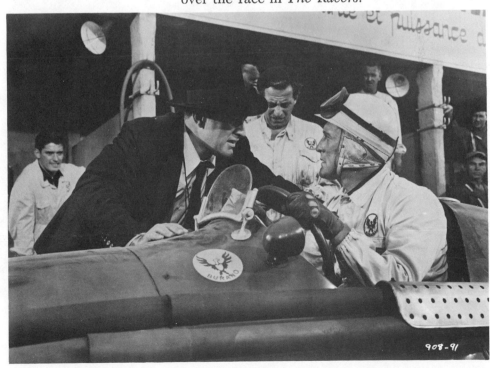

Pat Boone meets a skeptic in *State Fair*.

Nearing the finish line in *State Fair*.

Scene from *The Young Racers*.

Mark Damon and Luana Anders inspect a car in *The Young Racers*.

Starting line for a film entitled *Teen-age Mother*.

Actor or race driver? Both. It's Steve McQueen. That's a Formula Junior Cooper he's driving.

8

Is Truth Stranger than Fiction?

Lord Byron wrote: "Truth is stranger than fiction."

Some critics say movies have sometimes turned the tables with fictional happenings that looked plenty truthful.

With the car as a vessel of wrath or righteousness, love or hate the screen has preached some of the most exciting sermons on what to do and what not to do in both the back and front seats—epilogued with the rumble when it was in fashion . . .

Carol Channing, Barry Nelson, Ginger Rogers, and horseless carriage.

Russian star Nazimova exits from her electric.

Gladys Brockwell has engine trouble and Francis MacDonald comes to her aid.

Dame May Whitty ponders hitchhiker
Richard Cromwell from electric car.

John Wayne and Maureen O'Hara out
for a spin in a 1914 Stutz Bearcat.

Anne Little tries to escape villain.

Jack Mulhall shows off his 1918 Stutz.

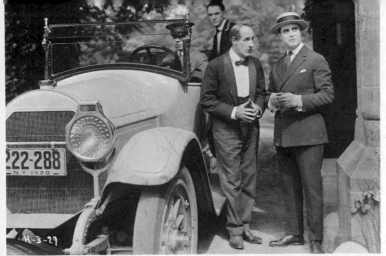

George Walsh seems slyly confident the lady is waiting, despite the dubious look on the butler's face as his chauffeur waits in 1919 Locomobile.

Vera Reynolds poses prettily in front of 1924 Dodge roadster.

Some of the best fights that boys have gotten into over girls have taken place in cars, as in this scene from a silent. The car on the left is a 1925 Flint.

A rumble seat was a spot for that shy guy in most of Harry Langdon's comedies—at least when Vernon Dent was at the wheel.

Warner Baxter tips hat in scene played against back of Signal Hill oil wells, which gushed millions for Hollywood stars who believed all gold was not yellow.

As *Sabrina* lovely Audrey Hepburn looks royal even when standing barefoot alongside a 1926 Rolls Royce. John Williams is hosing the car down.

James Stewart may be driving a 1926 Pierce Arrow, but he seems headed for trouble. (At right is a 1931 Chevrolet panel truck.)

Estelle Taylor wastes little time in showing Ronald Colman how she feels about a ride in a 1927 Hispano-Suiza in *The Unholy Garden*.

Anthony Dexter, in *Valentino*.

Cowboy giant Hoot Gibson in 1927
Cadillac.

Joan Crawford seems little concerned
over sleeping chauffeur, while Nils
Asther seems ready to raise cain in
Dream of Love. The dozing man is taking his nap in a 1927 Hispano-Suiza.

"Where's the Groom?" might be the
question. (The car: a 1929 Cadillac.)

Andy Devine and Irene Dunne pause,
in their 1929 Lincoln, for a chat.

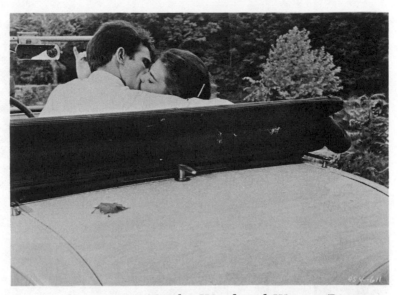

Natalie Wood and Warren Beatty as lovers in *Splendor in the Grass* make the front seat comfortable enough.

Gary Cooper shows off his 1930 Lincoln to Sylvia Sidney.

As *Bonnie and Clyde*, Warren Beatty
and Faye Dunaway use 1931 Plymouth
as shield.

Michael J. Pollard shoots it out, in
Bonnie and Clyde, behind overturned
1931 Graham.

Warren Beatty grapples; Faye Dunaway looks on. In the background is a
1930 Model A. The film, of course, is
Bonnie and Clyde.

Ramon Novarro and Madge Evans
Huddle in 1931 Chrysler.

Rex Harrison and Jeanne Moreau are about to leave for Ascot in *The Yellow Rolls Royce*. It's a 1933 model.

Posed alongside a 1932 Duesenberg, Elizabeth Taylor tries to understand a confused James Dean, in *Giant*.

It's getting pretty crowded in *About Face*. Foreground: 1936 Buick. Left: 1932 Ford.

Joan Blondell and Roland Young in *Topper Returns*. Eddie (Rochester) Anderson is the chauffeur, and Carole Landis is in the back seat of the 1937 convertible.

Alan Ladd and Dorothy Lamour talk things over over a 1937 Plymouth in *Wild Harvest*.

Linda Darnell and Paul Douglas team up in *The Guy who Came Back*. They prove that a back seat is perfect for settling most problems.

A lady waits alongside a 1940 Buick in *The Young Philadelphians*.

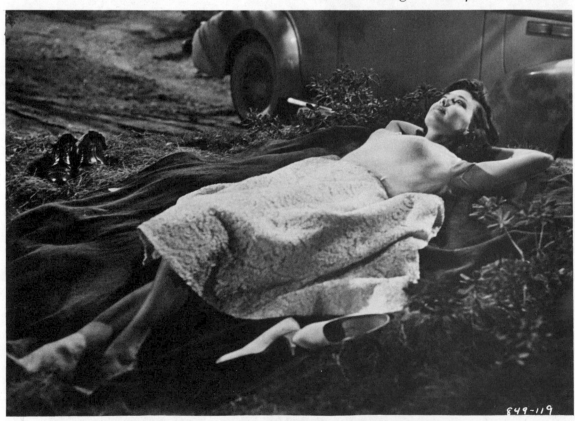

849-119

George Raft lights up for Ida Lupino
in *They Drive by Night*.

Robert Horton and Joan Leslie in a
1941 Buick.

Betty Grable, Carole Landis, and Victor Mature in *I Wake up Screaming*. The car is just a movie mockup.

The Navy knows the only way to "sail" on land is on wheels, as Tony Curtis and buddies show in *So This Is Paris*.

Carole Landis, Martha Raye, Mitzi
Mayfair, and Kay Francis are *Four Jills
in a Jeep.*

The Army also knows its wheels, as
only Dean Martin and Jerry Lewis could
prove in *At War With the Army.*

John Wayne, Claudette Colbert, and Don Defore seem overly pleased at a gassing up in *Without Reservations*.

James Stewart and Astrid Allwyn inside a Cadillac in *Mr. Smith Goes to Town*.

Gene Autry is smiling, but Lynne Roberts seems mad, in front of their 1946 Lincoln, in *Saddle Pals*.

Charles Coburn and Ella Raines in a scene from *Impact*. The 1946 Chevrolet cannot go any further.

Pat Boone leaps out of his 1947 Ford in *April Love*.

Ray Milland and Arlene Dahl in a
1950 Singer in *Jamaica Run*.

Frank Sinatra and Carolyn Jones in a
clinch for *A Hole in the Head,* which
may be a misleading title for romantics.
They are inside a 1957 Buick, which isn't
going to be going anywhere for awhile.

A lady doesn't wait in *Angel Baby*
starring Salome Jens and Burt Reynolds.
The car on the left is a 1952 Nash.

Troy Donahue and Diane McBain find grass greener in *Parrish*. Troy's 1955 Thunderbird is parked behind the lovers.

Elvis Presley and Tuesday Weld face a crisis in a garage for *Wild in the Country*. The car is a 1960 Chrysler.

Paul Newman and Joanne Woodward try to illustrate the title of their film, *A New Kind of Love*.

A collision between a Spyker (right) and an M.G. (left) in *Genevieve*, starring Dinah Sheridan and John Gregson.

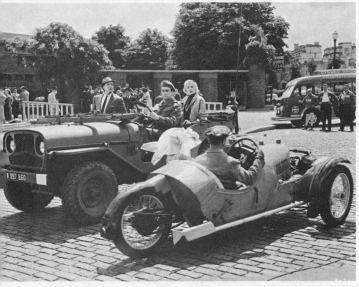

Gene Kelly eyes a three-wheeled Morgan in *The Happy Road.*

Carroll Baker seems more interested in her ice cream cone than in a ride with Karl Malden in *Baby Doll.*

In *Bus Stop,* Marilyn Monroe and Don Murray found excitement, and eventually love.

Eddie Fisher's Plymouth was a special
model for *Bundle of Joy*.

Rita Hayworth as *Gilda* about to hop
a ride with Glen Ford, at the wheel of
an M.G.

174

Marlene Dietrich outglamorizes a Rolls for her cameo role in *Paris When it Sizzles*.

That famed commercial, "It's a Ford," might apply here except it's that famed Hollywood couple, the Burtons, in a dramatic scene from *The Sandpiper*.

9

Behind the Camera

Here Hollywood's most guarded secrets are exposed.

Snowstorms made by wheels with fans.

A girl crashing into a tree.

A back seat faked.

De Mille making history in a back seat.

The wheels wait for the filmakers to manufacture their dreams for the celluloid . . .

Cecil B. DeMille directing a scene from back seat of Thomas studio car in 1916.

Two mesh-covered fans with 10-foot blades, mounted on old automobiles whose motors furnish their power, begin to whirl man-made snowstorm as Indians pass camera.

A typical set in the early days.

A reference still: Left, 33 Packard. Right, 1930 Model A.

Reference still: A typical old time gas station.

Reference still: Pierce Arrow, 1933.

Reference still: A Yellow Cab.

Comedy producer Al Christie beside a 1913 Model T loaded with bathing beauties.

The 150 beautiful girls who comprise the permanent chorus for Warner Brothers musicals arrive for work in a White Bus for *Show of Shows*.

Chic Sale and Jackie Cooper ride to set for their scene in a 1924 Lincoln.

In their 1933 Buicks, the Beverly Hills police for the first time have sending as well as receiving sets. The girl is Jean Chatburn, then an MGM featured player.

Early day Hollywood car showroom with what looks like a lady salesman for Ford (1933).

Small town scene in *Dr. Socrates*. Cast is lined up for bank holdup.

For a scene in *Singapore Woman*, Brenda Marshall was thrown in the water by David Bruce. Afterward the repentant Mr. Bruce offered Miss Marshall his assistance as a hair brusher. The truck is a 1935 Ford.

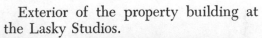

Character actor Otto Kruger inside
1946 Ford mockup.

Exterior of the property building at
the Lasky Studios.

Adolph Menjou talks over back-seat close-up with director Malcolm St. Clair, and famous cameraman James Wong Howe. The car is a 1928 Rolls Royce.

TRAVELER MEETS TRAVELER—Bob Burns meets the Arkansas Traveler, thereby clearing up a mystery. Bob thought he was the Arkansas Traveler, but he found out that the official one, appointed by the Governor of Arkansas, is a young fellow by the name of John G. Lonsdale, Jr. He was Bob's guest on the set where Burns was filming *I'm From Missouri*. Photo shows Bob taking Lonsdale's picture outside the soundstage. Lonsdale drives a 1939 Buick with a special license plate struck off by order of the governor.

Test Pilot director Victor Fleming discusses scene with Gable and Myrna Loy, who are inside a 1935 Ford.

Claire Trevor's wild flight from her killer husband in Twentieth Century Fox's *Big Town Girl* ended at this tree, where she swerved to avoid a herd of cattle on a lonely country road. The car is a 1931 Marmon.

This is how scenes were made for Richard Dix's *Sporting Goods*. In the front seat are Dix and Gertrude Olmstead; in the rumble, Myrtle Stedman. Director Malcolm St. Clair stands on the camera platform and Scenarist Tom Crizer (in the grey trousers) stands by to offer gags. (The car is a 1928 Rolls.)

Horse and carriage try to outstrut 1934 De Soto Airflow for fun during MGM lunch hour.

Paramount's *Those Were the Days* deals with college life, *circa* 1905. Director Ted Reed, to give players a taste of how they used to make pictures, reversed his cap, donned leggings, found a megaphone, and went into action. William Holden examines an ancient camera. (Paramount photo by C. Kenneth Lobben.)

Melvyn Douglas and Lila Lee in mockup shot.

Mildred Harris, Charlie Chaplin's first
wife, rehearses scene in 1929 La Salle
with camera mounted in the seat of a
1926 Packard. Behind them is a 1930
La Salle.

Director Jack Conway watches Robert Montgomery do a scene for *The
Truth Game.*

Director W. S. Van Dyke, in Africa for the filming of *Trader Horn,* stands on 1927 Packard.

A Willys Knight (1924) brings home the King of the Beasts.

Bathing beauties cluster around a 1934 De Soto Airflow, at Santa Monica beach.

10

Is There a Second Greatest Love?
The Little Man Asked

Most everyone knows the gags about seconds.

Can there be seconds in love?

In Europe and other places they are fashionable and called mistresses.

Is a Rolls Royce a second?

America is less romantic and realistic and so the courts take over in a charade called "divorce." They are listed by numbers and you can get any number for anything—not slicing the bread thin enough, etc.

Strangely enough back-seat driving is low on the list.

But for real lovers of wheels there is both affection, thrill, and sometimes tragedy. Some have died wheeling.

What more can you ask of love? . . .

Roscoe Arbuckle's Cars

As Minta Durfee Arbuckle recalls her husband's second greatest love:

"Roscoe hated riding on street cars, at that time we didn't have money to buy a bicycle. But dear Mack Sennett let him use either of the studio's two stand-by cars when available. One morning Roscoe trolleyed it to the fun factory in a fury. That night he rushed into the house to show me our first wheels—a Stevens-Duryea.

"Number 2 was an Alco made only for executives of that company.

"Number 3 was a big red MacFarland.

"Number 4 was his first Cadillac.

"Number 5 was a Renault.

"Number 6 was a large White—not a steamer.

"Number 7 was a Cadillac town car—Chauffeur-driven—it was the first of its kind at $9,000.

"Number 8 was a custom-built Hudson limousine.

"Number 9, I shall never forget. Returning from personal appearances in New York I met him at the train. He kissed me and ran down inside the long line of sleepers. Gone almost an hour I suddenly saw him driving the most beautiful imported Rolls Royce ever. Jumping out he grabbed me in his arms and sang, "Happy Birthday." Letting me down he said, 'Put your pretty fanny behind that royal wheel and tell them all to go to hell.' That was my Roscoe.

"Number 10 was a Pierce Arrow, his last golden wagon that didn't lead to the stars . . ."

Roscoe pretends woe sitting on fender.

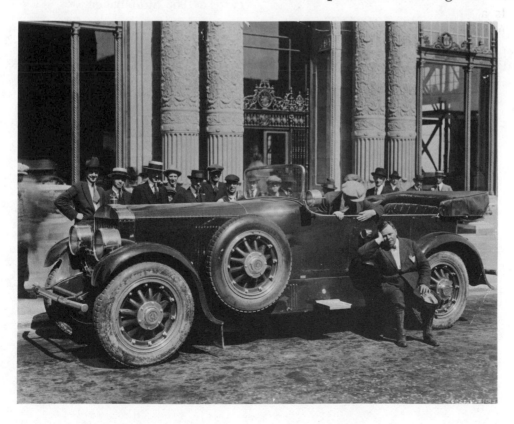

Fox film starlet and "The General"
go for a spin in a 1930 Bantam, one of
America's first compacts.

One-of-a-kind makes two when the
other one is Lauren Bacall. The unique
car is a 1953 Studebaker.

Lionel Barrymore alongside a 1935 Oldsmobile.

A 1928 Model A Ford Cabriolet acts as a background for some bigwigs of the silent era. Left to right: Monta Bell, director; Erich Von Stroheim, director; Carl Laemmle, Jr., general manager; and Robert Harris, assistant producer and head of scenario department at Universal Studios.

Richard Boone and his two favorites:
a Devin, *circa* 1959, and a filly who re-
fused to give her age.

Mary Brian.

A 1934 Chrysler waits to act in an
MGM movie.

The Jackie Coogan mansion on Oxford
Drive always sported two Rolls Royces,
according to Mrs. Lillian Bernstein, his
mother. On the street is a town car and
in the driveway a touring car, the favorite of Jack Sr. Both are 1924 vintage.

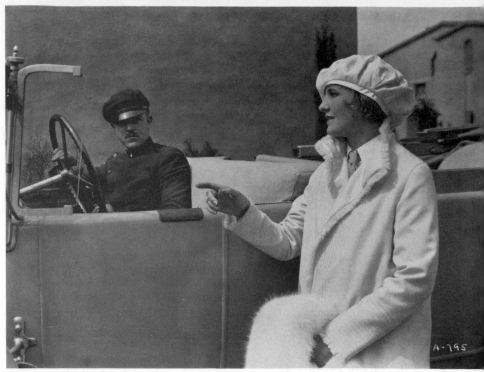

Maria Corda directs her chauffeur a[s] she starts for a location trip.

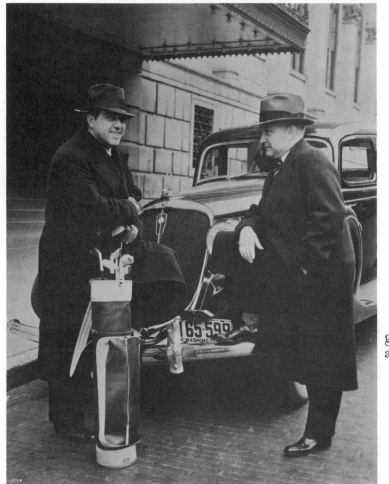

Opera star Richard Crooks out for golf with his 1934 Studebaker President and friend, at right.

Viola Dana pauses while trying to breathe life back into a flat tire.

Hal Cooley and a 1920 Kissel.

Lily Damita at the wheel of her 1929
Packard.

Lily Damita decorates a 1932 Packard
town car.

arion Davies (under table), Marie
ssler (right), and Dell Henderson
nter) wait for cameraman to line up
ot.

James Dean beside the 1954 Porsche
Spyder in which he lost his life.

This 1919 Locomobile was built for General Pershing to use in France, but the war ended before it was shipped across. De Mille bought the chassis for $12,500 and had the body made in California.

C.B. gives instructions to chauffeur beside 1922 Lincoln limousine.

Mr. De Mille and Adolph Zukor in 1919 Locomobile in front of Lasky Studio on Vine Street.

Mr. De Mille and Paramount Studio starlet in 1936 Cord.

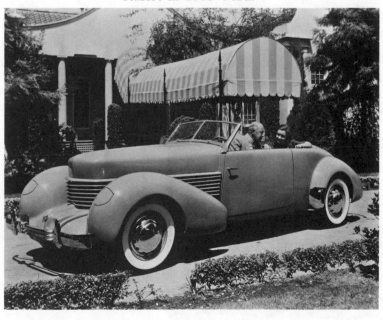

Mr. De Mille and seven-passenger custom-built Cunningham Eight.

Comedy stars Vernon Dent (center) and Charlie Chase (right) with friend before Vernon's 1918 Nash.

Walt Disney looks very debonair in a
1936 Packard.

Walt Disney standing beside the
"Cammione He," a cut-down ambulance
which he drove in France during World
War I. Actually, the car is a 1918 Model
T revamped for military use.

Walt Disney cuts a grass-caper at his fantasy factory.

Walt Disney and associate in conference beside his 1940 Packard Darin.

Jimmy Durante and friends with 1911
Ford.

W. C. Fields on golf course, hitched
to a 1935 Lincoln.

W. C. Fields tries to look the man-about-town beside his 1935 Lincoln.

Julia Faye, a De Mille starlet, beside a 1931 Cadillac V-16.

Clark Gable drives starlet Ann Morriss around MGM lot in 1940 Packard Darin on her first day of work.

Hoot Gibson also loved wheels that flew. Note his 1928 Rolls at left.

Hoot Gibson returns from a hunt in his 1928 Auburn Boattail Speedster.

Character actor Charles Grapewin beside 1937 Pontiac.

Director Edmund Goulding backs out
his 1926 Packard.

Hoot Gibson and famed animal trainer
Clyde Beatty stand in front of 1937
Studebaker. Two more Studes (1938 and
1939) are parked behind them.

Laurence Gray's 1926 Packard.

Comedy star Raymond Hatton shows pride in his 1928 A Model Cabriolet, one of the first in the film colony. Note the monogrammed radiator cap.

Cowboy great W. S. Hart stands between stage coach and his 1919 Locomobile.

Famous comedy director-actor Dell Henderson, at left, arrives, with his party, in Hollywood in a 1911 Packard.

Jack Holt entering his 1930 Buick.

With Hedda Hopper as passenger, singer-actor James Melton shows off a 1910 Stanley Steamer. A 1940 Packard Darin is parked alongside.

Silent star Gareth Hughes (right) shows his Willys Overland, 1918, to a friend.

A 1928 Buick seems to have upset William Jacobs.

German-born Emil Jannings, who won the first Academy Award in 1928 for his performance in *Way of All Flesh*, going for a jaunt in a 1927 Lincoln.

Al Jolson beside his 1928 Mercedes SPL, built especially for him.

Buster Keaton and sons Joe and Bob
go for a spin in a 1928 American Austin.

Sir Harry Lauder in 1914 Ford Model
T, which sold for $550.

Character actor Ben Lesley and starlet work on a 1933 Plymouth.

Elmo Lincoln, the first movie Tarzan,
at the wheel of a 1917 Metz.

Harold Lloyd relaxes on a 1946 Ford.

L. B. Mayer and his wife in back seat
of their first car, a 1910 Model T.

Steve McQueen and wife Neille about to blast off in a Ferrari.

Tom Moore and his daughter alongside a 1919 Hudson.

Tom Mix held a steering wheel almost as much as the reins. This is a 1920 Stutz.

Character actor Frank Morgan luxuri-ates in a 1933 Duesenberg—a car only for the rich.

Comedy queen Polly Moran and son
"take five" on a 1932 LaSalle, behind
which is a 1930 Model A.

Director Fred Niblo and his wife pose
with their 1923 Cadillac.

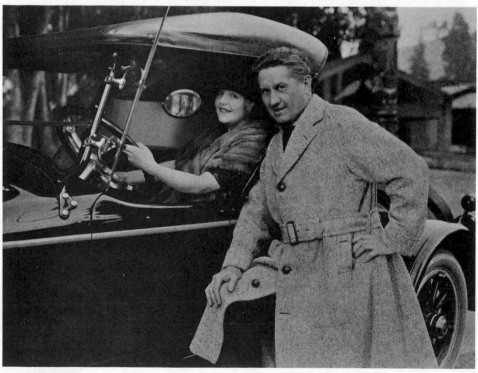

MGM featured player Edward Norris enjoys the power of his 1938 Packard Cabriolet 120.

On location in Europe, Merle Oberon poses in front of a Mercedes limousine. The car had once belonged to Nazi Foreign Minister von Ribbentrop, and was a duplicate of the one that Hitler used.

Mary Pickford and brother Jack chat
over lunch with director William Beau-
dine. A 1922 Rolls is parked behind
them.

Dorothy Sebastian does a little primp-
ing in a 1930 Chrysler.

Martha Raye and David Rose race back to Hollywood in 1931 Packard after their surprise elopement.

Dick Powell learns the law in 1934 Chrysler Air Flow.

English star Peter Sellers shows off
his 1933 Morgan.

Gloria Shea, Paramount starlet, sits on
her 1936 Chevrolet for a publicity shot.

MGM-13951

Norma Shearer demonstrates her portable dressing room for the camera.

One of Gloria Swanson's many cars (1921 Cadillac) outside one of her many homes.

Alice Terry enjoys morning ride to MGM studio.

Olive Thomas and a 1919 Stutz roadster.

Screenwriter Wanda Tuchok rides into Hollywood in a 1927 Nash.

Rudolph Valentino's Italian-built 1925 Isotta Fraschini.

Pearl White and her 1917 Rolls.

Jay Wright is all smiles with his 1933 Ford Roadster. In the background are a 1929 Du Pont (far left) and a 1934 Ford.

Loretta Young switches means of transportation, as she enters a 1932 Buick.

Rudolph Valentino's French-built 1925 Avion Voisin.

Johnny Weissmuller greets a visitor on the MGM lot while making *Tarzan Escapes*. They are standing in front of Johnny's 1933 Cadillac.

11

Where Did the Golden Dust Blow?

As Kings raced their golden chariots into battle and Emperors paraded their triumphs in jeweled carriages, movie stars of the silent screen took up the tradition and bronzed the Hollywood landscapes with the most elegant automobiles of the times.

But the glittering era is only a memory now, and though filmland is still a golden empire the tradition in both living and driving has passed.

What happened to these motored gems?

A few were salvaged by sentimental lovers of the past. Most ended on the junk heaps, not unlike some of their owners.

But James Brucker, a rancher from Camarillo, California, began wondering about these classic cars and what had become of them. If found, could they be salvaged? Beginning as a hobby, his interest expanded to the point where he would buy any car with a memory.

With thousands of dollars worth of wheels on hand, the problem of how to continue his hobby without starving generated a most unique business. He formed the Picture Car Company, with Jerry Ross as manager and chief mechanic, and began renting his historic automobiles to films and television.

Among those now appearing before the cameras:

A 1908 English Unic cab.

A 1914 Lozier worth $6,500.

A 1927 Rolls Royce owned by producer Joseph Schenck and his star-wife, Norma Talmadge. (Brucker bought it for $750. Ross worked nine months on its rehabilitation, and it is now a rare beauty valued at $6,000.)

Cecil B. De Mille's 1929 Lincoln Phaeton.

Charlie Chaplain's Piccadilly Roadster Rolls Royce, 1929 vintage.

Darryl F. Zanuck's 1938 to 1940 Cadillac Town Car.

Star Richard Arlen's 1930 Cadillac Phaeton.

The list has almost reached 500 and runs into thousands of dollars.

So where has the golden dust blown? Into James Brucker's pockets, film and television renters kid him. But Brucker's love of wheels has put him in the class of the art and book collector.

As he says of his charges:

"They are realities of a once precious dream that none of us can enjoy again . . ."

This 1930 Buick was used as Robert Stack's car in *The Untouchables*.

This 1930 Buick touring car saw service in *The Untouchables*.

This 1930 Cadillac roadster was seen
in *Harlow*.

A 1929 Rolls playboy roadster saw action in *Speedway*.

Joseph M. Schenck and Norma Tal-
mage used this 1927 Rolls town car.

These Cadillac town cars were built between 1938 and 1940. This one was Daryl F. Zanuck's.

Germany's 1936 Maybach appeared in the television version of *Twelve O'Clock High*.

This 1928 Chevrolet was seen in *To Kill a Mockingbird*.

A 1928 La Salle was part of the atmosphere in *The St. Valentine's Day Massacre.*

A 1927 Lincoln also saw service in *The St. Valentine's Day Massacre.*

Another featured car in *The St. Valentine's Day Massacre* was this 1929 La Salle.

An SSK Mercedes Boat Tail was seen in *Twelve O'Clock High*.

Alan Ladd displays a 1930 Cadillac Phaeton.

Robert Stack waits for action in a 1930 Studebaker, in this scene from *The Untouchables*.

Charlie Chaplin's Piccadilly Roadster Rolls Royce of 1929, updated in the early '30's. This photograph was taken at Pebble Beach, California. Receiving the award was James Bruckner.

And here, Stack salutes from a 1930 Buick.